THE UNTAMED WORLD

Blue Whales

Patricia Miller-Schroeder

RSVP
**RAINTREE
STECK-VAUGHN**
PUBLISHERS
The Steck-Vaughn Company

Austin, Texas

Published by Raintree Steck-Vaughn Publishers, an imprint of Steck-Vaughn Company.

Library of Congress Cataloging-in-Publication Data
Miller-Schroeder, Patricia.
    Blue whales / Patricia Miller-Schroeder.
        p.   cm. -- (The untamed world)
    Includes bibliographical references (p. 63) and index.
    Summary: Examines the life, environment, habits, and endangered status of the blue whale.
    ISBN 0-8172-4570-7
    1. Blue whale--Juvenile literature. [1. Blue whale.   2. Whales.
3. Endangered species.]   I. Title.   II. Series.
    QL737.C424M55   1998
    599.5'248--dc21   97-11465
                                                       CIP
                                                       AC

Printed and bound in Canada
1234567890 01 00 99 98 97

Project Editor
Lauri Seidlitz
Design and Illustration
Warren Clark
Raintree Steck-Vaughn Publishers Editor
Kathy DeVico
Copy Editors
Janice Parker, Leslie Strudwick
Layout
Chris Bowerman

Consultants
Catherine L. Berchok, formerly with the Mingan Island Cetacean Study, is now in the Graduate Program in Acoustics at the Pennsylvania State University.

Richard Sears is Director of the Mingan Island Cetacean Study. He has studied blue whales since the 1970s.

Acknowledgments
The publisher wishes to thank Warren Rylands for inspiring this series.

Photograph Credits
American Museum of Natural History: pages 52 (Neg. No. 337693 Photo. Hollenbeak and Beckett. Department of Library Services), 53 (Neg. No. 103586 Photo. Juluis Kirchner, Feb. 1918. Department of Library Services); **Frank S. Balthis:** page 36; **Tom Campbell's Photographic:** pages cover, 4, 16, 28 (Tom Campbell), 6, 30 (Peter Howorth); **Corel Corporation:** pages 7, 14, 17, 21, 23, 60; **Digital Stock Corporation:** pages 19, 43; **Greenpeace:** pages 40 (Morgan), 51 (Grace), 54 (Beltra), 55 (J. Meier-Wiedenbach); **Ivy Images:** pages 34, 37, 41 (Doc White); **Mammal Slide Library:** pages 8 (Dr. D.G. Huckaby), 12 (CETAP, University of Rhode Island), 15 (Dr. Emily Oaks); **New Bedford Whaling Museum:** page 61; **Richard Sears–MICS Photo:** pages 5, 13 (top), 13 (bottom), 18, 20, 22, 24, 26, 29, 32, 42, 57, 59; **Visuals Unlimited:** pages 10 (A. J. Copley), 45 (Bob Clay).

Every reasonable effort has been made to trace ownership and to obtain permission to reprint copyright material. The publishers would be pleased to have any errors or omissions brought to their attention so that they may be corrected in subsequent printings.

Contents

Introduction

Many people once thought whales were sea monsters.

Opposite: Blue whales are one of the great whales, a group of the largest whales in the world. Other great whales include right whales, gray whales, and humpback whales.

Whales have fascinated people for centuries. They were seen as mysterious creatures that lived under the waves far out at sea. Sailors told stories of their huge size and fierce nature. Many people thought whales were sea monsters. Today we still have a lot to learn about whales. One of the least known of these ocean giants is the blue whale.

In this book you will learn about the largest animal in the world. You will learn how creatures as large as a jet plane feast on tiny animals no bigger than your finger. Follow blues thousands of miles to warm seas where 2-ton (1,814-kg) calves are born. Learn how they keep in touch with one another over hundreds of miles (kilometers) of ocean. Read on to enter the watery world of the blue whale.

A blue whale swims by moving its powerful tail up and down in the water. When it dives from the surface, it sometimes raises its tail above water.

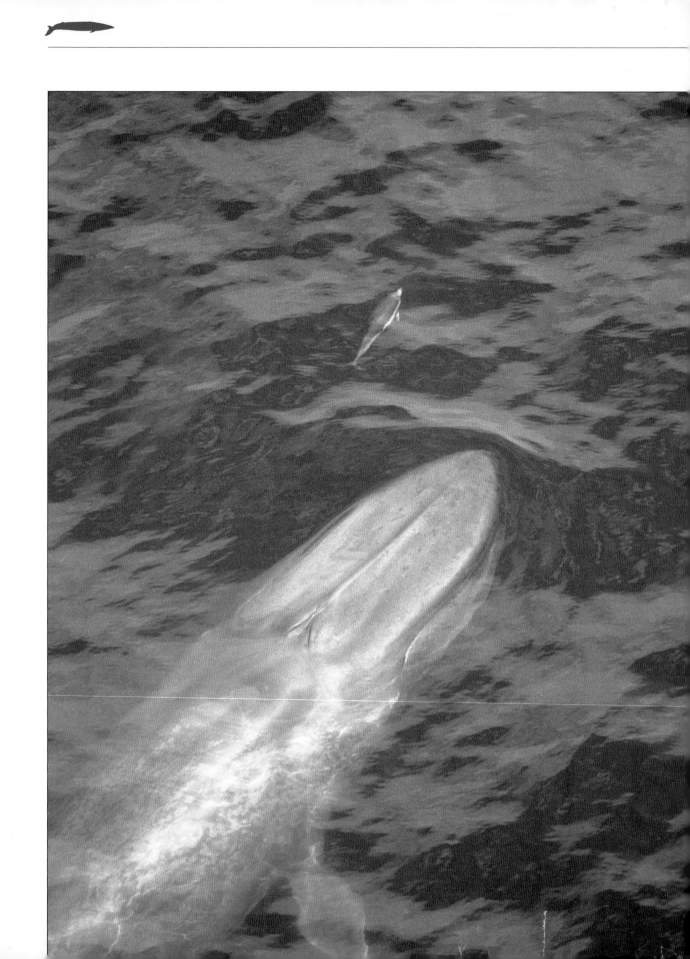

Features

*Opposite: Like blue whales, dolphins breathe through **blowholes**.*

Whales are a variety of sizes, from 6-foot (1.8-m) dolphins to the largest whale ever recorded, a 100-foot (30.5-m) blue whale. All whales are **streamlined** and well adapted for living in water.

Many people once thought whales were huge fish. Now we know that whales are not fish. They are mammals, like dogs, horses, lions, and humans. Like all mammals, they are warm-blooded creatures that breathe air. They also give birth to live young that drink milk from their mothers' bodies. Being a mammal poses special problems for an animal that spends its entire life in water. The blue whale, like all other whales, has solved these problems with many special features.

*Most often the only sight you will see of a blue whale will be a **spout** and maybe a back or fin.*

Whale Evolution

The ancestors of whales lived about 50 million years ago. These animals had four legs and lived on land. One group lived beside rivers near the sea. They began to spend most of their time in the water, hunting for food and avoiding predators. The first whales evolved from this group. Over millions of years, their front legs became **flippers**. Whale flippers still have finger bones. Their hind legs became smaller and finally disappeared. Today, however, a few whales are sometimes born with tiny, useless legs. Strong tails developed for swimming. Jaws became longer, which moved their nostrils to the tops of their heads. This made breathing at the water's surface easier. Many of these first whales became extinct. Modern whales appeared about 20 million years ago, probably evolving from a common ancestor.

Although a whale's flippers are now designed for steering through water, they still have the finger bones of their land-dwelling ancestors.

Classification

Blue whales have many relatives. There are about 78 species of whales and dolphins. They all belong to the order of animals called the **Cetacea**. The Cetacea is divided into two suborders. These are the toothed whales and the baleen whales. Baleen whales do not have teeth, although they are born with tiny tooth buds that never grow. Scientists believe this is evidence that toothed and baleen whales have evolved from a common toothed ancestor. Toothed whales catch and eat fish and squid. Baleen whales filter small creatures from the water with their huge mouths.

Blue whales are baleen whales. Blues are part of a group of baleen whales called **rorquals**. The rorquals are among the fastest whales in the oceans. They all have a pleated throat pouch that expands when they are feeding. Other rorquals are the fin, sei, Bryde's, humpback, and minke whales.

There is only one species of blue whale. Its Latin, or scientific name, is *Balaenoptera musculus*. Some scientists recognize a smaller subspecies called the pygmy blue whale, or *Balaenoptera musculus brevicauda*.

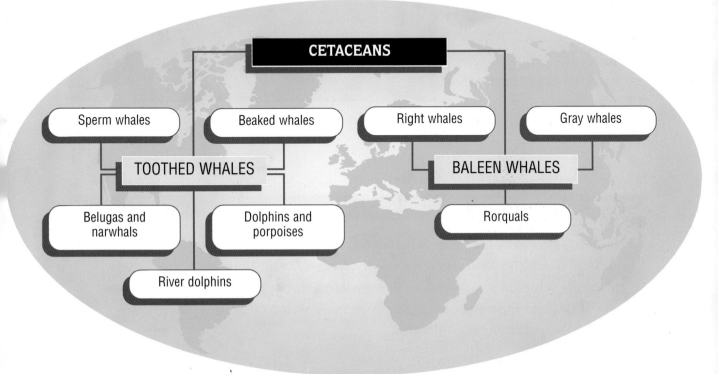

Size

Blue whales are the largest animals in the world. The largest blue whale ever recorded weighed more than 150 tons (136,000 kg). This is bigger than 30 full-grown elephants. Only one dinosaur, the seismosaurus, may have been larger. However, most of the really big blues were killed by whalers. The average size of blue whales today is around 70 to 85 feet (21.3 to 25.9 m). No one knows for sure how big they can grow.

Blue whales are big on the inside as well. A blue's heart is the size of a sports car, and its arteries are as large as drainpipes. Its tongue weighs 4 tons (3,628 kg) and is strong enough to hold an adult elephant.

Blue whales can grow to this enormous size because they live in the ocean. The water helps support their large weight. A blue whale will die if it is stranded on land. Its bones cannot support its body and will collapse, crushing its internal organs.

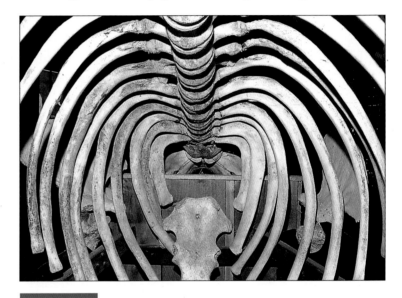

The skeleton of a blue whale can weigh more than 50,000 pounds (22,680 kg).

LIFE SPAN

No one is sure how long blue whales live. Some experts estimate that they live 60 to 70 years, but their life span may be longer. Adult blue whales and their calves are sometimes attacked by killer whales. Some are injured by collisions with ships, and others get entangled in nets. A serious threat to blue whales comes from pollution and oil spills.

Whale Researchers Talk About Blue Whales

Roger Payne

"When you are in the water and see a blue whale pass very close, it's a bit like standing on a train platform watching the train go by, hoping that the wind isn't going to suck you under its wheels."

Roger Payne is one of the world's leading experts on whales. He is president of the Whale Conservation Institute and is a scientific adviser to the International Whaling Commission. He has led over 100 ocean expeditions and has studied all species of large whales. He has written many scientific articles on whales and a book called *Among Whales*.

Erich Hoyt

"Often another blue is seen a kilometer or more away from a lone blue. Maybe blues, the largest animals on Earth, simply live life on a much bigger scale. Their low blasts carry easily for kilometers underwater. Perhaps they are all in close touch, or as close as they need to be..."

Erich Hoyt is one of Canada's top nature writers. He has written many articles on whales and several books, including *Meeting the Whales*. He is also a member of the Society for Marine Mammalogy.

Richard Sears

"Because of the nomadic nature of their existence, blue whales will, for a long time to come, reserve many surprises for those who study them. The parameters of their lives will be difficult to define, and this may be what appeals to those of us who study them."

Richard Sears has been studying blue whales since the 1970s. He directs studies of blue whales at the Mingan Island Cetacean Study on the St. Lawrence River in Québec, Canada, and in the Sea of Cortez, Mexico. He was the first to discover how to identify individual blue whales.

Special Adaptations

A whale spends its whole life in the ocean. It has more special adaptations for living in water than any other mammal.

Streamlined Bodies

Despite their large size, blue whales are slim and streamlined. Their smooth, torpedo shape and powerful muscles let them glide easily through the water. One of the fastest of the great whales, blues can reach speeds of 30 miles per hour (50 kph).

Skin

Whale skin is smooth and rubbery. It has few hairs, and its surface is covered in oil. This helps whales slide through the water. Blue whale skin is a spotted blue-gray color. A blue's underside is lighter in color and sometimes has a yellow tint. This yellow color comes from an alga that grows in cold water. The alga attaches to the whale's skin, giving its underside a yellowish color. Whalers who saw dead blues floating upside down gave them their nickname from this color—sulfur-bottoms.

A whale's powerful tail propels its streamlined body through the water with ease.

Blubber

Just beneath their skin, blue whales have a thick layer of fat called blubber. Blubber helps to keep whales warm. This is important because animals lose heat 25 times faster in water than on land. Blue whales put on blubber when they feed in the **polar oceans**. This is a good way to store food during their long **migrations**, when they eat very little.

About 15 percent of blue whales raise their tail flukes high above the water before diving deeply. Most other rorquals, like the fin, sei, and minke, rarely do this. Only humpback and right whales are commonly seen raising their flukes when they dive.

Flukes

The whale's powerful tail is made of two **flukes**. The tail is flat and rigid and lies horizontally. It moves up and down when the whale swims. This motion moves the whale through the water. Fish's tails are vertical and move from side to side. The huge flukes of blue whales are usually 18 feet (5.5 m) across.

Fins and Flippers

In some ways, whales resemble fish. Both have pectoral fins. In whales, the sturdy pectoral fins are called flippers. They help the whale steer through water. Like fish, whales have dorsal fins. The dorsal fin is a raised ridge on a whale's back made of a tough, fibrous material. It is visible above the surface when a whale comes up for air. Unlike a fish's fin, the whale's dorsal fin is hard and rigid. The dorsal fin of a blue whale is quite small in comparison to its huge size.

A blue's pectoral fins help it steer through water.

More Special Adaptations

Blowholes

A whale breathes through nostrils on the top of its head. The blue whale, like all baleen whales, has two openings. Toothed whales have only one. These openings are called blowholes because they are used to blow out old, stale air from the whale's lungs. This air comes out in a fine, misty spray called a spout, or a blow. Blue whales' spouts can blow 30 feet (9.1 m) into the air.

The blue whale's spout is taller and thinner than the spout of most other whales. It is also very loud.

Eyes

The eyes of blue whales are about the size of grapefruits. Although this sounds very large, it is actually quite small in relation to the whale's body. Whale eyesight is probably as good as human eyesight. However, because the water they swim in is often murky and dark, other senses such as hearing are more important than sight.

Touch

Most whales seem sensitive to touch. They often touch or rub against one another using their mouths, flukes, flippers, or whole bodies. Whales may rub against one another during play or mating. They also ram each other or hit with their tails or flippers when showing aggression.

Baleen

Like all baleen whales, blue whales do not have teeth. Instead they eat with the help of a special substance called **baleen**. Baleen is made of strong **keratin**, which also makes up human fingernails and hair. It grows in long strips from the whale's upper jaw. The strips fit closely together and are lined with bristles. When the whale gulps water into its mouth, the baleen acts like a filter. The whale then closes its mouth, forcing the water out through the baleen strips. The bristles trap anything that is too large to fit through the filter. This is how blue whales trap the tiny **krill** they eat.

blue whale
baleen

In different species of whales, the baleen strips vary in size and color. A blue whale has over 300 stiff, black baleen strips in each side of its mouth. The blue whale's baleen grows up to 3 feet (.9 m) long and has very fine bristles. The longest baleen strips belong to the right whale and may be up to 16 feet (4.8 m) long.

The baleen from whales was often used to make brushes, combs, umbrella ribs, and ladies' corsets.

Hearing

Hearing is the blue whale's most important sense. Whales do not have external ears. Their inner ear, or bulla, sits in a ball of spongy bone. This bone is not attached to their skull. Instead it is surrounded by a bubbly foam. Water is a good conductor of sound. For a whale to hear, sound waves must travel through the water and enter the whale's jaw. Vibrations are then carried to the bulla floating in its foam. Whales can hear so well underwater that people sometimes say whales can see with their ear.

Social Activities

The great whales live a long time, so studying their family life can take decades.

Opposite: Scientists who study whale social behavior must usually watch from the surface of the water. This limits their opportunities to understand complex behavior that happens underwater.

Most of what we know about whales has been learned from dead whales. A great deal is therefore known about their physical features. Much less is known about their social behavior. Scientists have started some long-term studies on whales living in the wild. These studies are giving a fascinating look into the lives of many species of whales. Most studies of whales have been on toothed whales such as dolphins, killer whales, and sperm whales. A few studies have now begun on some of the baleen whales.

The great whales live a long time, so studying their family life can take decades. The longest running study on blue whales is now taking place along the St. Lawrence River in Québec, Canada. Scientists there have photographed over 350 individual blues and are learning how to tell them apart. Other studies on blue whales are being done in the Sea of Cortez, Mexico, and off the California coast. So far, however, the social relationships and mating behavior of blue whales are mostly unknown.

Some whales, like killer whales, live in social groups called pods.

Social Group Composition

Many of the toothed whales studied appear to be very social creatures. They live in groups or families called pods. The blue whale, however, seems to be quite solitary. Outside of the mother-calf bond, little has been learned about relationships among blues.

Observers have often noted two blues swimming quite closely together. These pairs are normally within 50 to 100 feet (15.2 to 30.5 m) of each other, although the distance can vary a lot. Some pairs have been seen up to a mile (1.6 km) or more apart. The pairs may be related individuals, such as siblings, or two mates. A few may be mothers and calves. No one knows for sure. Sometimes several blue whales will be found feeding on a large school of krill. These may be only temporary groups gathering at a good food source. Scientists have observed 15 to 30 blues in a 5- to 10-square mile (13- to 26-sq km) area.

Because they are so huge, it is likely that each whale needs a large feeding area to itself. It is possible that during the feeding season the whales must spread out to get enough to eat. Once they migrate to their breeding area, no one knows if larger groups form. They do not eat much during this time, so they could form larger groups. However, they may stay scattered on the breeding ground with only mates coming together.

Although observers can sometimes see two whales swimming close together, they cannot always tell whether the whales are related.

Whale Social Behavior

Scientists have observed many social behaviors in different species of whales. The following are examples from two of the blue whale's relatives:

Sperm Whales

Female sperm whales and their calves live together in large nursery groups. Many of the females return to the same nursery group each year. The females in the group babysit for one another. When one female dives deeply to feed on squid, other females protect and care for her calf. Male sperm whales visit the nursery groups infrequently.

Humpback Whales

Male humpback whales compete for females by singing songs. All males sing a similar song when they begin their migration from the feeding grounds. By the time they arrive at the breeding grounds, the original song has evolved into a new one. Each male makes changes to the song and sings it slightly differently. The males sing for hours, repeating the beautiful, eerie notes over and over in order to attract females. They will continue the same song until the next year's migration from the feeding grounds. Humpback males will also compete aggressively for females. A male that is traveling with a female may drive off other males that come too close. He will sometimes strike them with his head or tail, or with his powerful flippers, which are covered with sharp barnacles. Barnacles are small marine animals that attach themselves to moving hosts.

Humpback whales are often covered with barnacles. Blues move through the water too quickly for many barnacles to latch on.

Communication

Some whales, like the humpback, communicate with long, complicated songs. Some toothed whales can hear and send ultrasonic sounds. These sounds are too high-pitched for humans to hear. Scientists think that blue whales also have many ways to communicate with one another across long distances. They make a variety of clicking and moaning calls. They also make noises by forcing air out of their blowholes or by slapping the water with their flippers or flukes.

Blue whales communicate with one another through a series of low-pitched moans.

Blue whales make low-pitched moans. These are deep and complex sounds. They may be the loudest and lowest in the animal kingdom. The moans last from 15 to 38 seconds. They are carried through the ocean for hundreds of miles (kilometers). Low frequency sound travels well in the ocean. The speed of sound in the water is 5 times faster than in air. The returning echoes may tell the whales where islands, shorelines, or other animals are located. The sounds may also be heard and answered by other whales. This may be how whales that are far apart keep in touch. Scientists are not sure what blue whales are communicating with their calls. Some think they may tell one another about the location of good food sources, such as a school of krill. Others think they warn of danger or keep a widely spaced group together.

Blue whales probably use sound to help them find food. Unlike dolphins, they do not use true **echolocation**. However, either the sounds the blues make or the sounds made by their food may guide them as they travel through the ocean.

Signals and Body Language

Many whales share certain signals and behaviors that are likely important in communicating. These behaviors are learned and practiced in play by young whales. Blues have not been observed in some of these behaviors as often as other whales. Breaching is the most commonly observed behavior in blues, and even it is rare to see.

Spyhopping

Most whales stick their head above the surface of the water. This is called **spyhopping**. It lets them look above the water's surface. They may be checking to see where other whales are and what they are doing. Sometimes they may just be curious about a boat or something else above the water's surface.

A breaching bottlenose whale

Lobtailing

Lobtailing is when a whale raises its tail fluke out of the water and splashes it down on the surface. This may have more than one purpose. Some toothed whales use it to herd fish. Other whales may use it to signal others or show aggression.

Flippering

This is a common activity and may be done with lobtailing. The whale lies on its side and raises a flipper above the water's surface. The flipper is then used to strike the water several times, causing noisy splashes.

Breaching

When a whale leaps out of the water and lands with a splash, it is called **breaching**. This is often done when other whales are nearby. Many young whales start breaching when they are only a few weeks old.

Whale Calves

Like most mammal infants, a whale infant depends on its mother for food and protection.

Opposite: Scientists now think calving grounds in the Pacific may be off the coast of Baja, in Mexico, and from the Sea of Cortez to the waters off Costa Rica. The sight of the blue whale's spout is often observed in this area.

Many land mammals are born helpless. They may be safely hidden in nests or carried by their mothers to protect them from harm. Whale infants, however, must be active and alert from birth. They need to be able to swim and follow their mothers. They have a lot to learn, and they must learn it quickly. The blue whale calf and mother spend most of their time alone. They may occasionally be joined by other whales. Scientists do not know how adult blues treat calves on the calving grounds. They do know that the bond between mother and infant is strong. Like most mammal infants, a whale infant depends on its mother for food and protection.

Most young Cetaceans, such as these Fraser's dolphins, are born into the security of a pod or family group. The number of animals in a pod varies a great deal by species.

Blue whales can be seen together during the mating season.

Mating and Birth

Blue whales mate during their winter breeding season. This is likely to be November to February for whales that live in the northern hemisphere and May to August for whales that live in the southern hemisphere. Biologists do not know if a blue whale female mates with just one male or many. Blue whales have occasionally been seen traveling in pairs. However, sometimes partners in the pair change. Because of this, scientists do not know if blue whales are **monogamous**. Whale experts now believe blues may be monogamous for short periods of time.

Both females and males are ready to mate when they are about ten years old. Females give birth to one calf every 2 or 3 years.

The **gestation** time for blue whales is 11 or 12 months. Pregnant whales leave their polar-feeding grounds and travel to warmer waters to give birth. When the mothers reach the calving grounds, a single calf is born. Blue whale calves are the largest infants in the animal kingdom.

Giving birth to an air-breathing infant in the ocean causes special problems. Calves are born tailfirst and are pushed to the surface by their mothers. This helps the infants to take their first breaths. Calves can swim right after birth.

Care

A newborn blue whale is as big as many full-grown whales of other species. Despite its size, it depends on its mother for food and protection. Its baleen plates have not grown yet, so it cannot feed itself. For the next 8 months, the calf lives on its mother's milk. During this time, it stays close to its mother.

The mother produces milk in nipples that are hidden in a slit on her abdomen. The calf nurses every few hours by pushing its mouth against the slit. The mother's milk is very rich in fat and vitamins. The young whale grows quickly while it nurses.

For at least 6 to 8 months, the young whale depends on its mother to protect it from killer whales and large sharks. During this time, the calf learns how to feed, avoid predators, and communicate with other whales. It also begins to learn the long migration routes it will travel every year.

Whale milk is 40 to 50 percent fat. Cow milk is only 5 percent fat.

Development

Birth – 8 Months

At birth, a newborn blue whale is about 20 to 25 feet (6.1 to 7.6 m) long, and weighs about 5,500 pounds (2,495 kg). The calf drinks 50 gallons (189 l) of its mother's rich milk each day. While nursing it gains 200 pounds (91 kg) a day or about 8 pounds (3.6 kg) an hour. The infant's skin is the same blue-gray as an adult's skin. Each calf has a distinctive spotted pattern on its flanks that it will carry throughout its life. By taking pictures of these patterns, scientists have learned to identify many individual blue whales. A calf's skin may be wrinkled at first, but it quickly becomes smooth and sleek. Its dorsal fin may be rubbery and bent over, but it soon straightens out. The calf swims well and follows its mother everywhere. It playfully practices adult behaviors like breaching and lobtailing.

Every blue whale has a different pattern on its skin. Infants have the same pattern they will show as adults.

8 Months – 1 Year

By the time a calf is eight months old, it weighs 50,000 pounds (22,680 kg) and is about 50 feet (15.2 m) long. Its baleen plates have grown and it is fully **weaned** and eating krill. The calf has migrated long distances with its mother to and from the feeding grounds. After 8 months most calves are quite independent.

1 Year – 10 Years

By the end of its first year, a young blue whale is on its own, although it sometimes may travel within a mile (1.6 km) or so of its mother. It is still growing and gaining weight as it becomes an adolescent. During feeding season, the young whale puts on about 88 pounds (40 kg) a day.

10+ Years

The whale is now an adult and is ready to breed. By this time, most females are about 79 feet (24 m) long, and most males are 74 feet (22.4 m) long. Some of these young adults continue to grow. Few grow larger than about 92 feet (28 m) long.

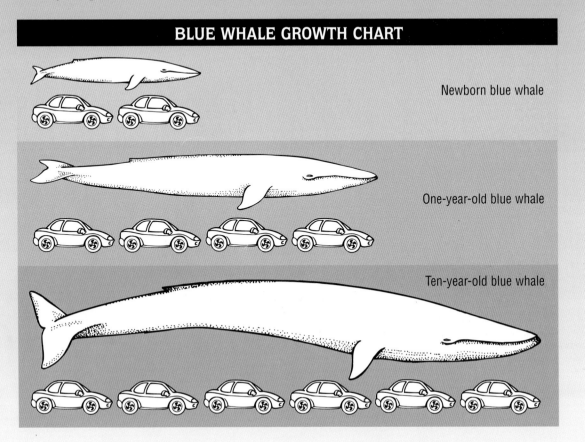

BLUE WHALE GROWTH CHART

Newborn blue whale

One-year-old blue whale

Ten-year-old blue whale

Habitat

Blue whales feed near the surface of the water. They are usually found within 300 feet (91 m) of the surface.

Opposite: Whales need air to breathe, so they can usually be found near the surface of their ocean homes.

Blue whales travel widely and can be found in a number of ocean environments. Part of their time is spent in the deep ocean. They can also be found in water close to shore and along continental shelves and ice fronts. Blues spend part of each year in cold Arctic or Antarctic water. They also spend part of their year in warm water near the equator.

Blue whales feed near the surface of the water. They are usually found within 300 feet (91 m) of the surface. Very rarely they will dive much deeper, up to 3,000 feet (914 m). This behavior has been noted in blue whales that are frightened or in pain, such as when they have been harpooned.

Blue whales can be found in cold and warm waters throughout the world's oceans.

A blue whale can travel at 30 miles per hour (50 kph).

Range

Blue whales wander freely over great distances in the oceans. They do not appear to defend a home range or territory. When several blues are in the same area, such as near a good feeding source, they space themselves out.

There are three main populations of blue whales. These are the North Pacific, the North Atlantic, and the Antarctic populations. The North Pacific and Atlantic populations are each probably split into eastern and western groups. The Antarctic blues can probably be split into groups that range on either side of South America, Africa, and Australia.

The rich feeding grounds of the Antarctic Ocean used to be where most blue whales gathered. Today perhaps only a few hundred blues survive in the whole southern ocean. There are still a few places where blue whales can be seen regularly every year. The best sites are in the St. Lawrence River in Canada and off the coasts of California and Mexico.

Whale-Watching

If you have the chance to take a whale-watching tour, you will want to be on the lookout for blue whales. From what you know of blue whale features and behavior, choose which of the following sights will likely mean you have spotted a blue whale.

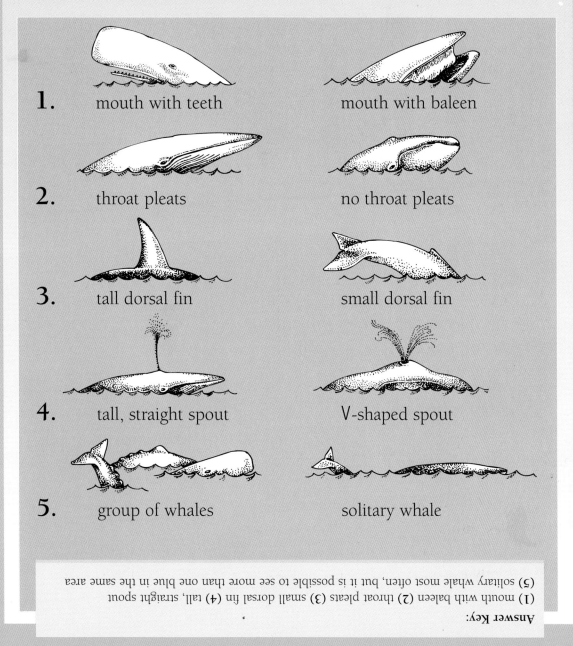

1. mouth with teeth — mouth with baleen
2. throat pleats — no throat pleats
3. tall dorsal fin — small dorsal fin
4. tall, straight spout — V-shaped spout
5. group of whales — solitary whale

Answer Key:
(1) mouth with baleen (2) throat pleats (3) small dorsal fin (4) tall, straight spout (5) solitary whale most often, but it is possible to see more than one blue in the same area

Migrations

The blue whale's year is divided between two main seasons: the summer feeding season, and the winter breeding and calving season. These two seasons are joined by long migrations. Whales that migrate to the northern hemisphere and whales that migrate to the south probably never meet. They are kept apart by continents and seasons. In April, the southern blue whales leave the Antarctic for warmer waters near the equator. They stay there until September, breeding and giving birth to their calves. At the same time that southern whales begin their journey north, northern whales leave the warm calving grounds. They head north for their feeding grounds in colder waters. Colder waters have more oxygen, which encourages animals such as plankton to grow. From October to March, the groups reverse their paths. The groups change territories at the same time, so it is unlikely that they ever occupy the same area at the same time.

How Do Whales Migrate?

When whales migrate, they must find their way across thousands of miles (kilometers) of open ocean. The same whales often return to the same place each year. How do they navigate and find their way? One theory is that they somehow use Earth's magnetic fields as a guide. Earth has regular patterns of magnetic forces that whales may have some way of receiving. They may use these patterns to navigate through the oceans. How they do this is another whale mystery we have yet to solve.

Blue whales have one of the longest migration journeys of any mammal—from the poles to the equator.

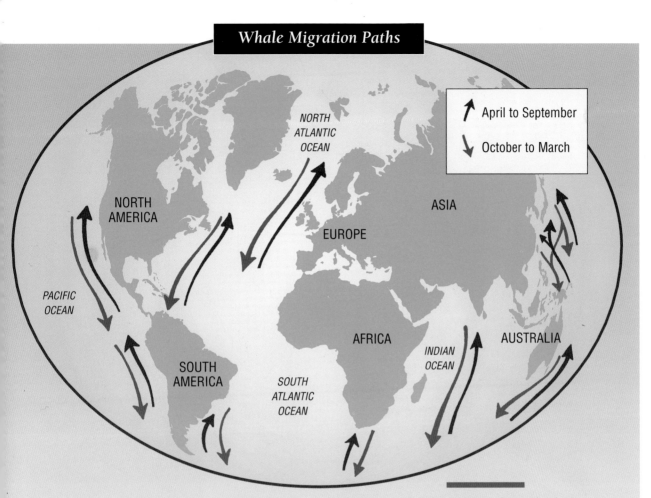

Whale Migration Paths

April to September

October to March

Scientists know the direction and time blue whales travel on their migrations. However, the actual migration paths are still a mystery.

Why Do Blue Whales Migrate?

Why do whales travel these great distances twice a year? Why do they leave rich feeding grounds and travel huge distances to places where there is less food?

Many scientists think the icy waters of the feeding grounds are too cold and stormy for calves. Others think that thousands of years ago the whales' feeding and calving grounds were closer together. Over time, changes in the ocean's temperature caused less food to be available in the warmer oceans. At the same time, more food became available in the colder oceans. The whales sought more abundant food sources in these areas. However, when it was time to mate or give birth, they traveled back to their familiar calving areas. Perhaps both theories are true. Scientists have seen blues feeding with young calves in the Sea of Cortez, a warm-water sea, so this migratory behavior may not apply to all whale populations.

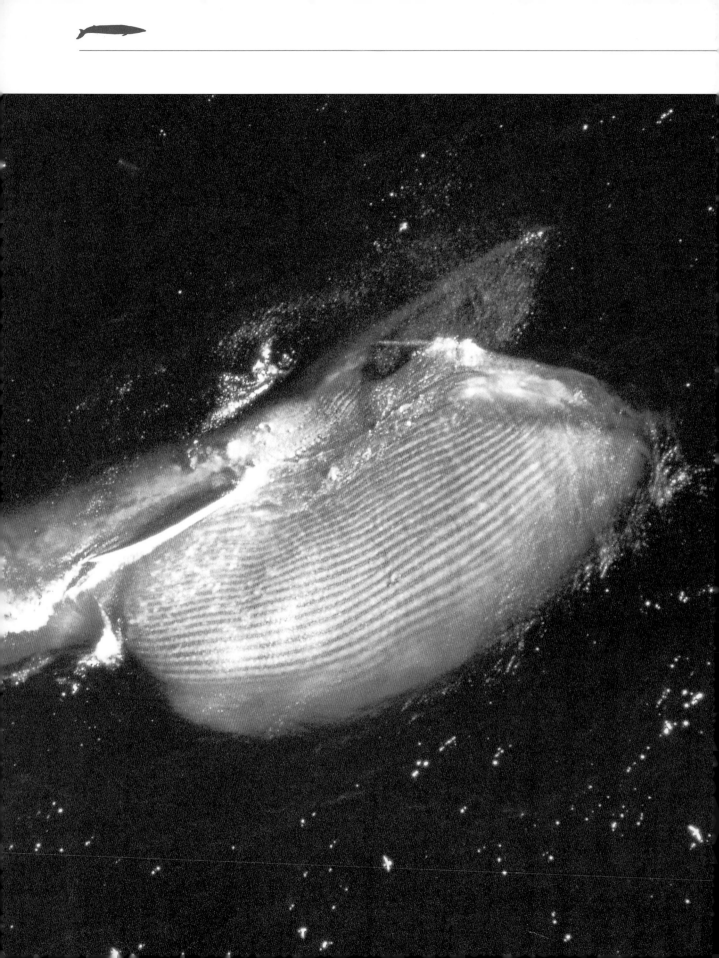

Food

Krill provide a rich source of food for many species of whales, seals, penguins, and seabirds.

Opposite: When a blue whale eats, its throat expands to take in tons (tonnes) of water and food.

The blue whale's favorite food is krill. The word *krill* means "whale food" in Norwegian. Krill are small animals that live in huge numbers in temperate, subtropical, and polar oceans.

Krill are members of a large group of very small marine animals called plankton. When they mate, krill form huge swarms that stretch for miles along the water's surface. They provide a rich source of food for many species of whales, seals, penguins, and seabirds.

Blue whales may sometimes eat small crabs and fish. It is likely that blues eat the fish that are also feasting on the krill when they move in to eat.

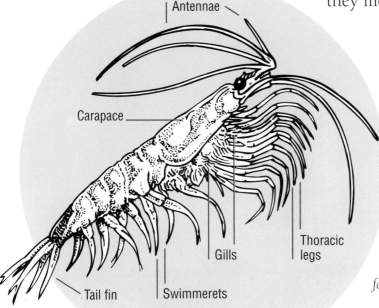

Antennae

Carapace

Gills

Thoracic legs

Tail fin

Swimmerets

Krill, measuring only 1 to 2 inches (2.5 to 5 cm) in length, are the main food of baleen whales.

What Whales Eat

Everything about the blue whale is big, including its appetite. To keep its huge body going, an adult blue whale needs to eat about 4 tons (3,628 kg) of krill a day. That is about 4 million krill a day for each whale during the feeding season. During this time, whales put on a lot of blubber. They may increase their weight by 40 percent.

However, when blue whales leave the feeding grounds, many do not eat much for several months. Blues will feed if krill is available on the calving grounds, but there is normally little food in the warm oceans. Many blues will go for long periods of time without eating regularly. Whales can do this and survive because the water supports their large weight. This means that they use very little energy to swim. In addition, whales are insulated by thick blubber. This means they do not use much energy to keep warm. Scientists now believe that some whales may stay in krill-rich waters all year-round.

When a whale eats fish, its excrement is brownish green. A diet of krill makes its excrement red.

How Whales Eat

How do blue whales eat such huge meals of krill? They have the help of the largest mouth in the animal kingdom. The jaws of an 80-foot (24.4-m) whale can be 22 to 24 feet (6.7 to 7.3 m) long. The blue whale has a muscular throat pouch that has folds of skin that look like pleats. The loose skin inside the pleats allows the throat to expand like a balloon while the whale is feeding. All rorqual whales have a pleated throat pouch.

When a blue whale finds a school of krill or other food, it opens its huge mouth wide. Its throat expands, and the whale gulps in water and krill. A blue may take in as much as 66 tons (59,862 kg) of water and food in one gulp. The whale then closes its mouth and contracts its throat pleats, forcing out the water through its baleen plates. The whale uses its tongue to help squeeze the water out. Anything too large to pass among the baleen plates is trapped. The whale then swallows the huge load of krill and other food trapped in its mouth. Each giant mouthful provides the whale with hundreds of pounds (kilograms) of krill.

After gulping a mouthful of water and food, a blue whale contracts its throat pleats and uses its tongue to push the water out. Baleen filters food from the escaping water.

The Food Cycle

A food cycle shows how energy in the form of food is passed from one living thing to another. Blue whales are carnivores, although the animals they eat are tiny. As they feed and move through the oceans, blue whales affect the lives of other living things.

Blue whales provide a home for "hitchhikers," such as barnacles and whale lice.

Blue whales are sometimes killed and eaten by killer whales.

Tiny plants and animals called plankton live in the ocean. They eat nutrients from the ocean floor in polar areas.

Small, shrimplike krill eat smaller plankton and are in turn eaten by blue and other whales.

When a whale dies, its body sinks to the ocean floor to add to the nutrients that cause plankton to thrive.

Viewpoints

Should krill, the major food source of many whales, be harvested to feed the world's hungry people?

Krill is a major food source for many marine animals. It is also the main food source for blue whales. Earth's human population is 5 billion people and still growing. Many people do not have enough to eat. Some experts suggest a major krill harvest as a way to feed many of the world's hungry. However, a commercial krill fishery would remove huge numbers of krill from the ocean. These krill would be removed from the food chains of the animals that depend on them, including blue whales.

PRO

1 Many of the world's poor cannot move to obtain more food. Animals such as blue whales are free to follow other food sources.

2 The number of whales living in the oceans has been greatly reduced by whaling. This reduced population does not need as many krill.

3 If the krill fishery is managed carefully and only excess animals are removed, there will be enough krill for animals and people.

CON

1 Animals have adapted over long periods of time to eating certain foods. They often cannot switch to another food source or change where they live or migrate.

2 Blue whales were almost destroyed by whaling. Their populations will not recover if their major food source is also destroyed.

3 Humans sometimes overfish and destroy fish stocks. This could happen with krill, destroying a major link in many ocean food chains.

Competition

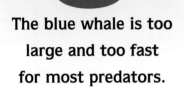

The blue whale is too large and too fast for most predators.

Opposite: Human use of the oceans as a dumping ground is now the blue whale's greatest threat to survival.

Blue whales have little to fear from most ocean animals. One blue whale can weigh as much as 30 elephants!

Blue whales may seem to have unlimited food and living space in the oceans. However, blues sometimes compete actively with other blues for food and mates. Blue whales have little to fear from most marine animals. They are too large and too fast for almost all ocean predators. Only killer whales hunting in packs and human whalers have been able to kill blue whales. Today it is humans' careless use of the oceans that is most threatening to the blue whale's habitat and food supply.

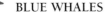

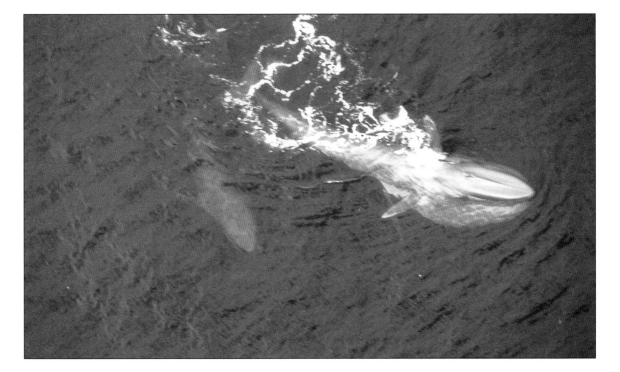

Blues feeding in the same area will space themselves out to avoid direct competition, if possible.

Competing with Whales

Researchers believe that blue whales must sometimes compete with one another for food and mates. However, such competition is difficult to measure, and may be too subtle for human observers. There are fewer than 8,000 blues living in the world's oceans, so competition may be unnecessary most of the time.

Blues share their feeding grounds with other whale species such as minke, fin, and humpback whales. Blues sometimes compete with these other whales, especially fins, for food. The fins' main diet is krill and other tiny, hard-shelled animals called crustaceans. However, most baleen whales feed on a wider variety of food than the blue whales, so they have more choice of things to eat. Blue whales avoid killer whales, which are their main ocean predators.

Relationships with Other Animals

The blue whale comes in contact with many other animals as it travels in the ocean. Many species of fish, dolphins, seals, and seabirds share the blue whale's home. The blue mainly sticks to its routine of feeding or raising calves. It leaves the other animals to go about their business in peace.

The blue whale itself provides a home for small creatures such as barnacles and whale lice. Barnacles cement themselves to the whale's skin. They travel with it and draw in food from the water. Whale lice look like tiny crabs. They dig into the whale's skin, feeding on it. The whale lice and barnacles do not really harm the whale, although they are likely irritating. Some humpback whales have been observed with raw chins after rubbing off barnacles. The blue is a fast-moving whale, so it does not have as many of these hitchhikers as slower whales, such as the gray and the humpback. Blues also sometimes give a little fish called the whalesucker, or remora, a ride. The whalesucker attaches itself to the whale's side and harmlessly travels with it.

The remora has a large suction cup on the top of its flat head so it can hitch rides from larger animals in the ocean. This remora is swimming under a jewel fish.

Folklore

Since ancient times, whales have been seen as mysterious creatures. Small whales, such as dolphins, often came close to shore. They were thought to be strange but friendly creatures. The large whales, however, were seen as dangerous sea monsters. They were only known from sailors' scary stories or when a dead whale was found onshore. A dead whale was often thought to be a bad omen. In many cultures, the large whales represented something to be feared and conquered.

Opposite: Early knowledge of whales came from sailors' stories of fierce sea monsters.

The sight of a dead whale on a beach can be shocking. The whale's massive size, normally hidden in water, is awesome onshore.

Folklore History

Whales have appeared in stories for more than 2,000 years. Aristotle, the Greek philosopher, recognized that whales were mammals 2,400 years ago. However, many ancient people believed whales were giant fish or sea monsters. Whales were often portrayed in pictures with huge, dragonlike mouths and tails. Stories were told of how whales would lure fish to their mouths with their sweet breath. Other stories were told of sailors mistaking whales for islands. When the sailors landed and made a fire, the whale would dive under the water, taking the sailors with it. Based on these tales, whales were thought to be animals that could not be trusted. They were seen as powerful enemies to be overcome. Killing a whale was considered heroic. It was not until the last few decades that people began to learn what whales are really like.

In Herman Melville's novel Moby Dick, *Captain Ahab searches the world for the* **albino** *sperm whale that caused him to lose his leg. Captain Ahab becomes obsessed with killing Moby Dick, and he dies in a dramatic fight with the giant whale. In real life, albino sperm whales are very rare.*

Myths vs. Facts

Whales are fierce creatures that will attack and destroy boats and people.

Whales are generally peaceful creatures that seem to be friendly to humans. They often seek contact with whale watchers or people in small boats. However, whales that have been harpooned or those whose young are threatened can be dangerous.

Whales such as the blue could swallow people because of their huge size and gigantic mouths.

The blue whale and other baleen whales are able to expand their huge throat pouches and take in tons (tonnes) of water at a time. However, their throat opening is very small. Whales would be unable to swallow something as large as a person. They would not be able to chew up a person either, because they have no teeth.

Whales must come up to the surface to breathe, so they do not sleep.

Whales do sleep, although how they breathe while sleeping is still unknown. One theory is that sleeping whales float near the surface of the water, taking catnaps between breaths. Another theory is that they may rest only one-half of their brain at a time while sleeping. The half that is not resting prompts them to breathe.

Folktales

You may enjoy reading some of the exciting stories that have been written about whales. The following are just a few. There should be more at your local library.

Ocean Life

The Twilight Seas is a story of the birth, life, travel, and adventures of a young blue whale.

Carrighan, Sally. *The Twilight Seas*. New York: Weybright and Talley, 1975.

In *Winter Whale*, a child is transformed into a humpback whale and experiences life in the ocean among whales.

Ryder, Joanne. *Winter Whale*. New York: Morrow Junior Books, 1991.

Whale Problems

The Prince of Whales is the story of a young whale attempting to carry on the ancient tradition of underwater singing, while struggling to survive against pollution and whalers.

Fisher, Robert. *The Prince of Whales*. New York: Quicksilver Books, 1985.

In *The Hostage*, a boy and his father capture a killer whale. The father plans to sell it to an amusement park, but the boy is not sure that this is the best thing to do.

Taylor, Theodore. *The Hostage*. New York: Delacorte Press, 1987.

In *Nobody Listens to Me*, a girl and her father both love whales but are in conflict over whale-watching after the death of a favorite whale.

Guccione, Leslie Davis. *Nobody Listens to Me*. New York: Scholastic, 1991.

People Swallowed by Whales

There have been stories of large whales swallowing people throughout history. In the following stories, the people survive and are either rescued or escape.

In the Bible, Jonah tries to hide from God on a fishing boat. God sends a storm, and the frightened crew throw Jonah overboard. He is swallowed by a whale and lives for 3 days in its stomach. After promising to do what God has asked him to do, Jonah is spit out, unhurt, onto a beach.

The ancient Greeks told a similar story. In their version, it is the mythical hero Hercules who is swallowed by a whale. After 3 days, he is spit out unharmed.

One nineteenth-century whaling story is about a whaler who was swallowed by a sperm whale. This man, too, was able to survive unharmed until the whale was killed and he was rescued several hours later.

In the modern fairytale *Pinnochio*, the wood-carver Gepetto and his wooden son, Pinnochio, are swallowed by a fierce whale. They are able to trick the whale into spitting them out unharmed.

Southern Ocean Whale Sanctuary

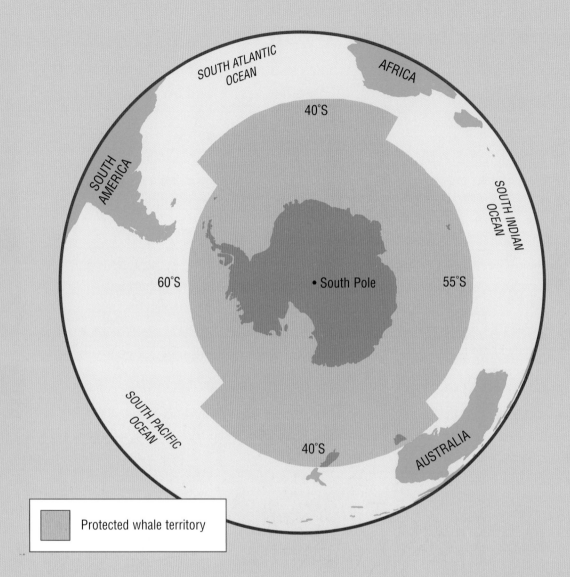

SOUTH ATLANTIC OCEAN

AFRICA

40°S

SOUTH AMERICA

SOUTH INDIAN OCEAN

60°S

• South Pole

55°S

SOUTH PACIFIC OCEAN

40°S

AUSTRALIA

Protected whale territory

In 1994 the International Whaling Commission declared most of the southern oceans a sanctuary for whales. The Southern Ocean Whale Sanctuary now protects whales in one of their most important feeding areas. Sperm whales and almost all baleen whales that live in the southern hemisphere migrate to these oceans to feed every summer.

Status

Scientists estimate there are only 4,000 to 8,000 blues left in the world.

Drift nets often accidentally kill whales, dolphins, sharks, and even seabirds.

The great whales were once abundant in every ocean of the world. Before modern whaling began, there were 250,000 to 300,000 blue whales. Today blue whales are endangered. Scientists estimate that there are only 4,000 to 8,000 blues left in the world. The greatest loss occurred in the southern oceans, where the population was once 200,000. The whales fed on rich stores of Antarctic krill. The whalers followed blues there, killing huge numbers of whales. Today fewer than a thousand blue whales remain in the southern oceans. Their numbers have not grown much in the 30 years that blue whales have been protected.

Whaling

Whales have been hunted by humans for over 2,000 years. Whale blubber was prized because it could be made into oil that was used to make soap, candles, and lipstick. Whales were also killed for their baleen. Baleen was used to make many items, such as brushes, corsets, and umbrella ribs. Baleen was once

Thousands of whales were once killed for their baleen, oil, and meat.

used for many things that are now made from plastic. Whale meat was used as pet food. Many people liked to eat it as well.

Early whaling was a dangerous business. Hunters paddled small boats right up to whales and tried to kill them with handheld spears and harpoons. Blue whales did not have much to worry about from this kind of whaling. They were too big and too fast to be hunted in this way. However, in the 1860s steam-powered boats and powerful, exploding harpoons began to be used. The tip of one of these weapons would explode like a bomb inside the harpooned whale. The whalers could now hunt with deadly efficiency.

Because of their huge size and thick blubber, blue whales became the whalers' favorite target. Whalers would need to kill only one blue whale to get about as much oil as 6 sei whales could provide. The whaling industry even had a unit of measure called the Blue Whale Unit. Each unit was the amount of oil an average blue whale could produce. The industry set limits on how much oil a whaler could take in a year in Blue Whale Units.

Stopping the Hunt

In less than 100 years of active hunting, the blue whale had almost disappeared. The Antarctic whale population was hit hardest, because it had most of the largest whales. By the 1960s, there were no longer enough blue whales left to hunt profitably.

In 1966 the International Whaling Commission (IWC) placed a worldwide ban on hunting blue whales. The IWC was formed in 1946 by the whaling nations. Its goal was to regulate the whaling industry by setting limits on the number of whales that could be killed each year. The IWC also placed bans on hunting whale species that were thought to be threatened.

In 1982 the IWC asked member nations to phase in an end to commercial whaling by 1986. Several countries at first refused to follow this decision. Iceland finally ended its whale hunts in 1989. Norway and Japan continue to hunt minke whales. Most whale meat is exported to Japan, where it is considered a luxury food.

This is a can of whale meat from 1918. Some countries still consider whale meat to be a delicacy. Demand for whale meat by Japanese shoppers supports most of the world's whale hunts.

New Threats

Today blue whales cannot legally be hunted. Whaling is no longer a threat to the blue whale's survival, although some whales may have been illegally hunted since 1966. Now there are new dangers. Human pollution of the oceans is the largest threat to blue whales. Toxic chemicals often end up in the ocean, where they poison the whales' food supply. When whales eat, the poison becomes concentrated in their bodies. Mother whales pass poisons to their calves through their milk. Whales may also swallow garbage floating in the ocean near their feeding areas.

Oil spills can pollute large stretches of ocean. The oil can cling to the whales' skin, making them sick. It also poisons their food and destroys their habitat. Many ocean animals die in oil spills.

The use of drift nets is another problem. Drift nets are up to 30 miles (50 km) long. Fishers drag these huge nets in the ocean, creating a death trap for many marine mammals. Drift nets are especially dangerous for calves, but even large whales can become trapped and drown. A young female blue whale was found dead after getting tangled in a fishnet in the St. Lawrence River in 1991.

Oil spills, toxic chemicals, and human waste are deadly threats to whales and other ocean animals.

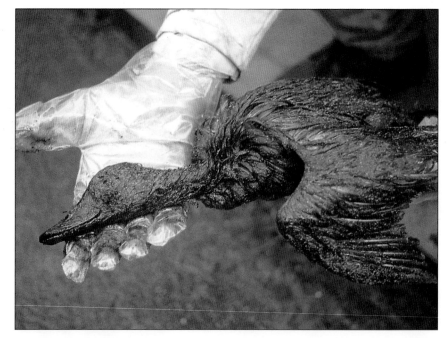

Saving the Whales

Whales became a symbol for the conservation movement in the 1970s. In 1971 a conservation group called the Animal Welfare Institute launched a worldwide Save the Whale campaign. This campaign encouraged people to boycott companies that used sperm whale oil to manufacture products. Another group called Greenpeace made worldwide headlines by intervening in whale hunts. Greenpeace activists would zoom in between hunters and whales in rubber life rafts. Public pressure forced many companies to find other products to replace whale oil. Oil made from the jojoba plant, a desert shrub, is now used as a replacement for whale oil.

Despite efforts to save whales, it may be too late for some species. Blue whales take so long to grow and reproduce that their populations may never recover from the whale hunts. Today's problems of pollution only further threaten the recovery of whale populations. A few populations may be increasing slightly, but their numbers remain very small. Scientists still have not seen a recovery of the blue whale population, even though legal hunting ended over 30 years ago. In places where the populations were greatly reduced, the blues may have a hard time even finding mates.

In April 1993, at a rally to save the whales, many children signed a large petition in Washington, D.C.

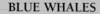

Viewpoints

Do whale-watching tours help whale conservation?

Whale-watching tours are popular with many people. Tours take groups of people out into the ocean to see whales close-up. A variety of boats are used, from small rubber life boats to large boats carrying 200 people or more. People taking the tours are thrilled and awed by their experience. However, some people complain that whale watchers harass the whales. They think that the tours should be stopped or kept from coming too near the whales.

PRO

1 People who see whales up close come away with a new respect and appreciation for whales. These people will want to help save whales from extinction.

2 Whale-watching provides income for people and communities. It shows those who used to depend on whaling that whales are worth more alive than dead.

3 Many whales seem to enjoy contact with whale watchers. They approach the boats and seem very curious. They may even present their heads or flippers for people to touch.

CON

1 You can appreciate whales from a distance. When you get too close, you may disturb them or even draw the attention of predators like killer whales to them.

2 The more thrilling the experience, the more money the tour operator makes. Some operators may be tempted to approach whales too closely and take risks in order to increase their profits.

3 Whale watchers may affect whale behavior and migrations in ways we do not yet understand.

In 1991 more than 4 million people spent a total of over $400 million to go whale-watching. This financial gain could help convince whaling nations to stop hunting whales and to start conserving them.

Adopt-a-Giant

The first long-term study of blue whales is being done in the Gulf of St. Lawrence, in Canada. The study is part of the Mingan Island Cetacean Study headed by Richard Sears. Sears and his research team have photographed and identified over 350 blue whales since 1979. They have learned that many of the same whales return to the St. Lawrence every year to feed. The research team is also studying blue whales in the Sea of Cortez, in Mexico. They have identified over 325 blues in that area.

You can help them learn about blue whales and become part of the research team by adopting one of the blue whales in their study. Whales may be adopted by school classes or by individuals. As a foster parent to a blue whale, you receive a photo and information about your whale. You also receive a newsletter about the work of the whale researchers. Most of all, you get to help blue whales through the research program.

For more information on the blue whale research program, or the "Adopt-a-Giant" program, contact the:

Mingan Island Cetacean Study
285 Green Street
St. Lambert, Québec
J4P 1T3
Canada

What You Can Do

Whales are fascinating animals that need your help. You can learn more about whales by writing to a conservation organization for more information.

Conservation Groups

INTERNATIONAL

Cetacean Society International
P.O. Box 9145
Wethersfield, CT
06109

Cousteau Society
930 West 21st St.
Norfolk, VA
23517

Whale and Dolphin Conservation Society
191 Weston Rd.
Lincoln, MA
01773

UNITED STATES

American Cetacean Society
P.O. Box 2639
San Pedro, CA
90731

Center for Whale Research
1359 Smuggler's Cove
Friday Harbor, WA
98250

Greenpeace
1436 U St. NW
Washington, D.C.
20009

CANADA

World Wildlife Fund Canada
90 Eglinton Ave. E.
Suite 504
Toronto, Ontario
M4P 2Z7

Twenty Fascinating Facts

1 The height and shape of each whale species' spout is distinctive. An experienced whale watcher can tell what kind of whale is below the surface by its "blow." The blow of a blue whale is a straight column, 30 feet (9.1 m) tall.

2 A small child could crawl through a blue whale's aorta, which is the main artery that carries blood from its heart to the rest of its body.

3 The tail fluke of a blue whale has many tiny blood vessels. These vessels work like a car's radiator to cool a hot whale.

4 Blubber thickness is one of the factors affecting how fast a whale can swim. Whales with very thick blubber, such as the northern right whale, cannot swim quickly, or their blubber insulation would cause them to overheat.

5 Blue whales have more blubber than many other types of whales. The most oil ever made from the blubber of one blue whale was 50 tons (45,350 kg).

6 Some whales like to "people watch." They approach boats to get a closer look at people. Calves may be especially curious. Blues do not do this as much as some other whales.

7 Whales evolved from the same primitive group of animals as deer and cows.

8 A blue whale's flippers are long, thin, and pointed, but they may look short and stubby because of the blue's large size.

9 Modern whale ancestors had hind legs. Whales are still sometimes born with a tiny pair of useless legs.

10 A whale's tail fluke does not show up in its skeleton because it contains no bone.

11 Cetaceans got their name from the Greek word *ketos*, which means "sea monster." The scientific name for toothed whales means "sea monsters with teeth." The scientific name for baleen whales means "sea monsters with mustaches."

12 The blue whale's two blowholes are protected by large, fleshy splash guards. Powerful muscles open and close the blowholes quickly so that no water gets into the whale's lungs.

13 Most information on whale sizes came from whales killed by whalers. Weights were estimated by weighing chopped-off chunks of meat and adding a few tons (tonnes) for lost blood.

Blue whale calves may seem to grow right before your eyes. Calves gain 8 pounds (3.6 kg) an hour while they are nursing.

 For whales, breathing is not automatic, like it is for humans or other mammals. Whales must think to breathe.

 A blue whale calf is as big as a full-grown elephant. When a blue is full grown, it is as big as 30 elephants.

 If a blue whale's intestines were stretched out, they would be as long as three football fields.

 Baleen was sometimes called whalebone. It was often used to make corsets. Corsets are rigid undergarments once worn by many women to make themselves look slim.

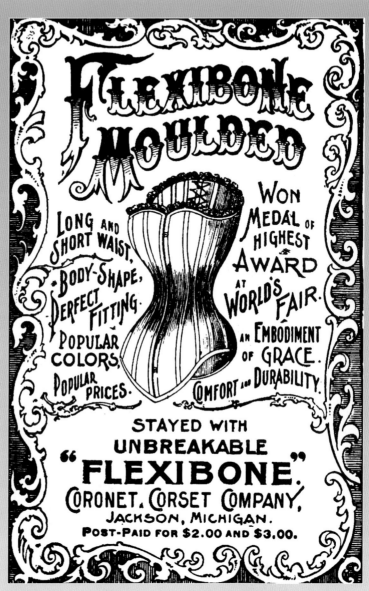

 When blue whales breathe, they empty out and refill 90 percent of the air in their lungs. Human beings only replace 12.5 percent of the air in their lungs with each breath.

 Baleen is made of keratin, the same material that is found in human hair and fingernails. Like nails and hair, it grows continuously, so worn-out baleen is simply replaced.

Glossary

albino: An animal lacking color in its skin, hair, and eyes

baleen: A strong plate of keratin, frayed on one edge, in the mouth of a baleen whale

blowholes: Nostrils on the top of a whale's head used to blow out stale air from the whale's lungs

breaching: Behavior in which a whale leaps out of the water and lands with a splash

Cetacea: The large order of animals that includes all whales and dolphins

echolocation: The use of reflected sound waves to locate food and other objects

flippers: Paddlelike forelimbs that help a whale steer through water

fluke: Two flukes form the whale's flat, rigid tail. The tail moves up and down to propel the whale through water.

gestation: The amount of time it takes for an animal to develop inside its mother's womb

keratin: Continuously growing substance that forms human nails and hair and the baleen of whales

krill: Tiny, shrimplike animals that are the main food of many whales and marine animals

lobtailing: Behavior in which a whale raises its fluke out of the water and hits the surface

migrations: Moving regularly from one area to another

monogamous: Having only one mate

polar oceans: Cold oceans near the North and South poles

rorquals: A special group of baleen whales with pleated throats that expand while feeding

spout: Misty spray blown into the air when a whale comes to the surface to breathe

spyhopping: Behavior in which a whale raises its head above the surface of the water to look around

streamlined: A simplified design to reduce resistance while moving through water or air

weaned: When a calf is no longer nursing on its mother's milk

Suggested Reading

Bailey, Jill. *Project Whale*. Austin, Texas: Raintree Steck-Vaughn Publishers, 1991.

Carrighan, Sally. *The Twilight Seas*. New York: Weybright and Talley, 1975.

Corrigan, Patricia. *Where the Whales Are*. Chester, Connecticut: Globe Pequot Press, 1991.

Ellis, Richard. *Book of Whales*. New York: Alfred A. Knopf Inc., 1980.

Hoyt, Erich. *Meeting the Whales*. Camden, Ontario: Camden House Publishers, 1991.

Papastavrou, Vassili. *Whale: Eyewitness Books*. Toronto: Stoddart Publishers, 1993.

Payne, Roger B. *Among Whales*. New York: Scribner Inc., 1995.

Index